U.S. POLICY TOWARD MOROCCO

HEARING

BEFORE THE

SUBCOMMITTEE ON
THE MIDDLE EAST AND NORTH AFRICA

OF THE

COMMITTEE ON FOREIGN AFFAIRS
HOUSE OF REPRESENTATIVES

ONE HUNDRED THIRTEENTH CONGRESS

SECOND SESSION

APRIL 9, 2014

Serial No. 113–134

Printed for the use of the Committee on Foreign Affairs

Available via the World Wide Web: http://www.foreignaffairs.house.gov/ or
http://www.gpo.gov/fdsys/

U.S. GOVERNMENT PRINTING OFFICE

87–518PDF   WASHINGTON : 2014

For sale by the Superintendent of Documents, U.S. Government Printing Office
Internet: bookstore.gpo.gov   Phone: toll free (866) 512–1800; DC area (202) 512–1800
Fax: (202) 512–2104   Mail: Stop IDCC, Washington, DC 20402–0001

COMMITTEE ON FOREIGN AFFAIRS

EDWARD R. ROYCE, California, *Chairman*

CHRISTOPHER H. SMITH, New Jersey
ILEANA ROS-LEHTINEN, Florida
DANA ROHRABACHER, California
STEVE CHABOT, Ohio
JOE WILSON, South Carolina
MICHAEL T. McCAUL, Texas
TED POE, Texas
MATT SALMON, Arizona
TOM MARINO, Pennsylvania
JEFF DUNCAN, South Carolina
ADAM KINZINGER, Illinois
MO BROOKS, Alabama
TOM COTTON, Arkansas
PAUL COOK, California
GEORGE HOLDING, North Carolina
RANDY K. WEBER SR., Texas
SCOTT PERRY, Pennsylvania
STEVE STOCKMAN, Texas
RON DeSANTIS, Florida
DOUG COLLINS, Georgia
MARK MEADOWS, North Carolina
TED S. YOHO, Florida
LUKE MESSER, Indiana

ELIOT L. ENGEL, New York
ENI F.H. FALEOMAVAEGA, American
  Samoa
BRAD SHERMAN, California
GREGORY W. MEEKS, New York
ALBIO SIRES, New Jersey
GERALD E. CONNOLLY, Virginia
THEODORE E. DEUTCH, Florida
BRIAN HIGGINS, New York
KAREN BASS, California
WILLIAM KEATING, Massachusetts
DAVID CICILLINE, Rhode Island
ALAN GRAYSON, Florida
JUAN VARGAS, California
BRADLEY S. SCHNEIDER, Illinois
JOSEPH P. KENNEDY III, Massachusetts
AMI BERA, California
ALAN S. LOWENTHAL, California
GRACE MENG, New York
LOIS FRANKEL, Florida
TULSI GABBARD, Hawaii
JOAQUIN CASTRO, Texas

AMY PORTER, *Chief of Staff*   THOMAS SHEEHY, *Staff Director*
JASON STEINBAUM, *Democratic Staff Director*

————

SUBCOMMITTEE ON THE MIDDLE EAST AND NORTH AFRICA

ILEANA ROS-LEHTINEN, Florida, *Chairman*

STEVE CHABOT, Ohio
JOE WILSON, South Carolina
ADAM KINZINGER, Illinois
TOM COTTON, Arkansas
RANDY K. WEBER SR., Texas
RON DeSANTIS, Florida
DOUG COLLINS, Georgia
MARK MEADOWS, North Carolina
TED S. YOHO, Florida
LUKE MESSER, Indiana

THEODORE E. DEUTCH, Florida
GERALD E. CONNOLLY, Virginia
BRIAN HIGGINS, New York
DAVID CICILLINE, Rhode Island
ALAN GRAYSON, Florida
JUAN VARGAS, California
BRADLEY S. SCHNEIDER, Illinois
JOSEPH P. KENNEDY III, Massachusetts
GRACE MENG, New York
LOIS FRANKEL, Florida

CONTENTS

Page

WITNESSES

Mr. William Roebuck, Deputy Assistant Secretary of State for Egypt and Maghreb Affairs, Bureau of Near Eastern Affairs, U.S. Department of State 6

Ms. Alina Romanowski, Deputy Assistant Administrator, Bureau for the Middle East, U.S. Agency for International Development 14

LETTERS, STATEMENTS, ETC., SUBMITTED FOR THE HEARING

Mr. William Roebuck: Prepared statement 8
Ms. Alina Romanowski: Prepared statement 16

APPENDIX

U.S. POLICY TOWARD MOROCCO

WEDNESDAY, APRIL 9, 2014

House of Representatives,
Subcommittee on the Middle East and North Africa,
Committee on Foreign Affairs,
Washington, DC.

The committee met, pursuant to notice, at 3 o'clock p.m., in room 2167 Rayburn House Office Building, Hon. Ileana Ros-Lehtinen (chairman of the subcommittee) presiding.

Ms. ROS-LEHTINEN. The subcommittee will come to order. We will sadly soon be interrupted for votes, but getting interrupted for democracy is a good thing.

After recognizing myself and Ranking Member Deutch for 5 minutes each for our opening statements, I will then recognize other members seeking recognition for 1 minute. We will then hear from our witnesses and without objection, the witnesses' prepared statements will be made a part of the record and members may have 5 days to insert statements and questions for the record subject to the length limitation and the rules. The chair now recognizes herself for 5 minutes.

With all the upheaval, instability, and social unrest in the wake of the Arab Spring, Morocco is designated as a major non-NATO ally and is working toward a political transition in instituting democratic reforms. Three years ago, King Mohammed proposed constitutional reforms that would push Morocco toward democracy and reform, shifting some power that was centralized in a monarchy to the people. This new constitution was ratified a few months later and was succeeded by parliamentary elections that saw a new government formed, complete with a new Prime Minister from an opposition party with a mandate to have more power to govern. Of course, the political situation in Morocco is still not perfect, but it is important for us to recognize the positive steps forward.

On the issue of the Western Sahara, long-standing U.S. policy, which I support, advocates for a solution based on a formula of autonomy under Moroccan sovereignty. While I recognize the advancement that the kingdom has made, when it comes to human rights, certainly more can still be done. According to the 2013 State Department Human Rights Report on Western Sahara, "The most important human rights problem specific to the territory was Moroccan Government restrictions on the civil liberties and political rights of pro-independence advocates."

(1)

Morocco has made strides in expanding women's rights and has created the National Council of Human Rights to evaluate all the human rights issues. As allies, we should work together as partners to accelerate their plans to implement the constitutional reforms that urge gender equality and parity. Since becoming the very first nation to formally recognize the newly independent United States of America, Morocco and the United States have shared a strategic and bilateral relationship. It is one that has continued to strengthen over the past few years as we have just seen Secretary Kerry return from a trip in which he took part in the second round of the U.S.-Morocco Strategic Dialogue aimed at deepening our bilateral cooperation on a variety of issues.

Our nation signed and implemented a free trade agreement nearly 10 years ago and there is certainly room to grow for both the Moroccan and U.S. economies through U.S. commercial investment and expansion of American businesses in the Maghreb. Last year, Morocco successfully completed a 5-year Millennium Challenge Corporation Compact in which the U.S. helped Morocco increase productivity, employment prospects, investment, and economic growth. MCC concluded that the results on the compact were impressive, given the complexity of the endeavor with tens of thousands, mostly women, learning to read and write through the literacy program.

So the political transition toward democracy is being paralleled by Morocco's economic transition which is under way. But that is contingent upon Morocco remaining a safe and stable country and that is yet another area in which our two nations collaborate closely. While the rest of the region struggles to cope with radicalization and Islamic fundamentalism, Morocco is working to foster and spread a more moderate form of Islam in the Muslim Kingdom. One way Morocco promotes religious moderation and tolerance is through its nearly 10-year-old program in which it trains women in Islamic theology right alongside their male counterparts, an idea that would not only be taboo in many other countries in the region, but would likely be highly illegal. While the kingdom has not been immune to the threat of home-grown extremism, Morocco is on the front lines of fighting terrorism throughout the region. Our two nations work closely in this regard and Morocco has proven to be an important ally.

One important counterterrorism effort that we can work closely with Morocco on is the Trans-Saharan Counterterrorism Program which aims to address the potential terrorist and security threats in Northwest Africa and the Sahel region, but we can and must do more. The administration must continue to see Morocco as the potential for what other North African transitional countries can do and we must look to glean the best practices from its approach and see how they can be implemented in neighboring countries as well.

And with that, I turn to my good friend, the ranking member, Mr. Deutch of Florida.

Mr. DEUTCH. Thank you, Madame Chairman. Thanks for holding today's hearing. Thanks to our witnesses for being here today to examine the long-standing United States-Morocco partnership. And when we say long-standing, we mean it as Morocco was the very first country to recognize a U.S. independence. It is nice to have Ambassador Bouhlal here as well. Thank you for joining us.

Last November, President Obama welcomed King Mohammed to the White House to affirm our strategic relationship and commit to strengthen and mutual cooperation on a host of significant issues. On the security front, Morocco has emerged as a critical partner in our efforts to fight extremism and promote stability in the Maghreb and in the Sahel. Morocco is one of only two African countries to be designated as a major non-NATO ally and is a member of the Global Counterterrorism Forum.

Just last week, the United States and Morocco concluded the annual African Lion joint military exercise with approximately 350 service members, 150 Moroccan Royal Armed Forces members and participants from various European African partners. This level of cooperation is paramount to confronting the threats posed by groups like al-Qaeda and the Islamic Maghreb and other al-Qaeda affiliated militias and to assist in our joint efforts to stem weapons transfers and narcotrafficking across the continent. It is clear that Morocco is committed to taking substantial action to prevent Northern Africa from becoming a safe haven for terrorist groups.

I would also like to highlight a unique initiative launched by the king to train imams from Mali, Tunisia, Libya, Guinea and the Ivory Coast and Morocco. It is my understanding that the first group of 100 imams have already arrived. This is a welcome approach to curbing the spread of extremist ideology in a volatile region of the world.

In addition to its leadership role on regional security matters, Morocco has pursued greater bilateral ties on economic and development issues with many of its African neighbors. In November, the king signed 18 agreements with Mali on a range of issues from microfinance to energy. But Morocco still struggles with its own economic development as the economy has been adversely affected by the economic troubles in Europe, Morocco's largest trading partner.

The 2011 expansion in state spending on social programs, public hiring, and subsidies has also put a strain on the economy. Unemployment rates among youths are estimated at 22 percent among males, and 38 percent among females. I am pleased that one of the pillars of USAID's new country development strategy signed in November 2013 is addressing youth unemployment.

Political reforms initiated by the king in response to unrest have seen success, and we must continue to help shepherd along reforms that will address civil society participation. USAID remains focused on helping to build civil society to include expanded roles for women in a political and economic space.

The United States has also contributed to Morocco's economic growth in a significant way through the completion of a $698 million Millennium Challenge Corporation Compact and the country has not been selected for a second compact.

Morocco has long played a leading role in fostering greater cooperation between North Africa and the Middle East, coordinating closely on farm policy matters with the Gulf Cooperation Council. As chair of the Al-Quds Committee and the Organization of Islamic Cooperation, we look to Morocco to play a positive role in helping to foster continued peace talks between the Israelis and the Palestinians. We cannot forget that it was King Hassan that in the 1980s took the bold step of inviting then Prime Minister Shimon Perez to Morocco for peace talks. In that vein, many of us were concerned to see a law proposed in Parliament late last year that would have criminalized any normalization of relations with Israel. I hope that we will not see any advancement of this proposal.

Finally, in advance of the king's visit last November, Chairman Ros-Lehtinen and I reiterated our support for the long-standing U.S. policy to support a solution to this dispute based on a formula of autonomy under Moroccan sovereignty. This policy has enjoyed the support of the last three administrations and continues to earn strong bipartisan support in Congress. With over 200 years of friendship between our two countries, the U.S.-Morocco partnership will only be strengthened by the launch of last year's strategic dialogue. As Secretary Kerry said last week during his visit, the strategic dialogue will contribute to the ability of the United States and Morocco to show that we value something a lot more powerful than our past and that is the future.

I look forward to hearing from our witnesses on how we can continue to help Morocco bolster its economic and security situation as we continue to enhance the U.S.-Morocco partnership. I yield back.

Ms. ROS-LEHTINEN. Thank you very much, Mr. Deutch and we would like to acknowledge the presence of the Ambassador of the Kingdom of Morocco to the United States. Thank you, Ambassador Bouhlal for being with us today. You are a dear friend. Thank you so much.

And now I am pleased to yield for his opening statement to the chairman of the Subcommittee on Asia and the Pacific, Mr. Chabot of Ohio.

Mr. CHABOT. Thank you, Madame Chair, and thank you for holding this hearing. We have witnessed political and humanitarian crises all around the world in recent times, but we don't hear that much from Morocco and maybe that is not a bad thing. We are looking forward to hearing from our witnesses today and getting an update on our current relationship with the kingdom and a status report on regional political situations.

We know that in 2011, King Mohammed responded to the ongoing Arab Spring by drafting a new constitution which was subsequently adopted by popular referendum that afforded new authority to elected officials. I hope our witnesses can speak to how that reform is being carried out.

Additionally, I hope our witnesses will comment on the performance of the Justice and Development Party and Islamist Party which in 2012 won the largest number of parliamentary seats in the Moroccan election. So there is a lot to talk about and so I will stop talking and I yield back and look forward to hearing our witnesses. Thank you.

Ms. ROS-LEHTINEN. Thank you so much, Chairman Chabot. And so pleased to yield to another Florida colleague, Lois Frankel for her opening statement.

Ms. FRANKEL. Madame Chair, it is a little lonely down at this end.

Ms. ROS-LEHTINEN. Come in closer, come on over.

Ms. FRANKEL. I will. First, thank you so much for being here. I am very interested in this, and Madame Chair, I have a number of questions, but I would like to hear our witnesses' testimony and then I will go forward with them.

Ms. ROS-LEHTINEN. Thank you very much.

Ms. FRANKEL. Thank you.

Ms. ROS-LEHTINEN. Now we turn to Mr. Cotton for any opening statement he would like to make. And the subcommittee is very pleased to have a special guest with us today, Mr. Grimm, who has been a long-time friend of Morocco and has been very much involved in their issues. Please give an opening statement if you could, Mr. Grimm.

Mr. GRIMM. Well, thank you so much, Madame Chairwoman. As the co-chair of the Congressional Morocco Caucus I thank you for holding this hearing and for inviting me to be with you today among my friends, so thank you. Morocco, it has already been said and everyone knows, has historically been one of America's strongest and most reliable allies. Currently, the Kingdom of Morocco is a strong partner in combatting terrorism throughout North Africa and Morocco is also the only country in the African continent in which we have a free trade agreement. So I think that is extremely important to note.

King Mohammed successfully weathered the Arab Spring mostly by listening to the Moroccan people and making appropriate reforms and for this I think he should be commended. As already mentioned, Madame Chairwoman, during President Obama's recent meeting with King Mohammed, they specifically pledged and I quote, ''A shared commitment to advancing the peaceful resolution to the Western Sahara issue based on autonomy under Moroccan sovereignty.'' Well, I believe that the United States Congress has a responsibility to assist Morocco in achieving this resolution. The State Department, USAID, and other development agencies in the United States Government must devote some of their assistance funds for Morocco to projects designed to improve the quality of life for the people of Western Sahara. So I am very excited to be here. I thank you again. And I am looking forward to hearing from our witnesses today. Thank you and I yield back.

Ms. ROS-LEHTINEN. Thank you so much, Mr. Grimm, and you are always welcome to come to our subcommittee. Thank you. And we are so pleased to welcome our excellent witnesses today. First, we welcome Mr. William Roebuck who is the Deputy Assistant Secretary of State for Egypt and Maghreb Affairs. Before this, he served as Charge d'Affairs in Tripoli for 6 months from January to June 2013 and as Director for the Office of Maghreb Affairs in the State Department's Bureau of Near Eastern Affairs from 2010 to 2012. Welcome, Mr. Roebuck.

We also have with us Ms. Alina Romanowski. Did I do that pretty well? I have got a difficult name so I don't worry if someone mispronounces mine. And Ms. Romanowski is currently Acting Assistant Administrator for the Middle East Bureau at the U.S. Agency for International Development. Prior to this position, Ms. Romanowski, and of course, Eddy would put her name in every sentence here, served as Deputy Assistant Administrator in the Middle East Bureau focusing on U.S. assistance programs in support of political transitions in Egypt, Libya, Tunisia, and Morocco. We welcome our witnesses and we will begin with you, Mr. Roebuck. Your prepared statements will be made a part of the record. Please feel free to summarize them.

STATEMENT OF MR. WILLIAM ROEBUCK, DEPUTY ASSISTANT SECRETARY OF STATE FOR EGYPT AND MAGHREB AFFAIRS, BUREAU OF NEAR EASTERN AFFAIRS, U.S. DEPARTMENT OF STATE

Mr. ROEBUCK. Thank you very much, Chairman Ros-Lehtinen, Ranking Member Deutch, members of the subcommittee, Congressman Grimm, thank you very much. I am honored to appear before you today to offer you these remarks on U.S. policy to Morocco. I am pleased to appear with my good friend, USAID Assistant Deputy Administrator Alina Romanowski. I have had the pleasure of working with Alina to further our foreign policy objectives in Morocco and in the region. We welcome the opportunity to speak to you today and look forward to answering any questions you might have about Morocco or our policy toward Morocco.

With your permission, I will request that my full statement be submitted to the record. So I will just summarize here briefly.

Madame Chairman, as you know, Morocco, as several of you have mentioned, is the first nation to have recognized the United States in 1777. It is an important and long-standing ally. We continue to enjoy a very strong bilateral relationship with Morocco focused on promoting regional stability, supporting democratic reform efforts, countering violent extremism, and strengthening trade and cultural ties. We worked to strengthen our relationship with Morocco during the November 2013 visit of King Mohammed VI to Washington. This visit provided an opportunity for the United States to affirm our close strategic partnership with Morocco and to discuss the best means of promoting security and prosperity in the region.

We continued our conversations during the recent U.S.-Morocco Strategic Dialogue which Secretary Kerry opened in Rabat on April 4th. This Dialogue was originally launched 2012 and it discussed new avenues for cooperation in the political, security, economic, educational, and cultural spheres. We are also very pleased that our new Ambassador to Morocco, Dwight Bush, was confirmed in March and has arrived in Rabat.

Regarding briefly democratic reforms in Morocco, under King Mohammed VI, the Moroccan political system has gradually liberalized. A new constitution, as several of you noted, was adopted in 2011 and Morocco's first Islamist-led government won nationwide democratic elections. The country moved forward in 2013 with calibrated, but steady, political and economic reforms. We have a robust dialogue with the Moroccan Government on human rights and on ways in which we can support this on-going process of political reform.

Our mutual concern for peace and stability in the region means that the United States and Morocco are fully engaged on both economic and security cooperation. On economic cooperation, USAID's new country development strategy directly addresses the issue of youth employment, a key driver of instability in the region through the creation of new vocational programs and career centers. The

United States and Morocco also recently held the second U.S.-Morocco Business Development Conference in Rabat with 58 American companies participating. Regarding security cooperation, Morocco is one of our closest counterterrorism partners. Morocco is an active member, as you have noted, of the Trans-Saharan Counterterrorism Partnership and also the Global Counterterrorism Forum.

Regarding Western Sahara, the United States supports the United Nations-led process designed to bring about a peaceful, sustainable, and mutually acceptable solution to the Western Sahara question. U.S. policy toward Western Sahara has remained consistent for many years. We support the work of U.S. Secretary General's personal envoy, former U.S. Ambassador Chris Ross in his efforts to find a mutually-acceptable solution.

Regarding education and cultural cooperation, the United States and Morocco have a long history of people-to-people ties. One recent example is Morocco's support of the J. Christopher Stevens Virtual Exchange Initiative. The initiative is designed to fuel the largest ever growth in people-to-people exchanges between the United States and the broader Middle East. And Morocco has graciously committed to donate $1 million per year over the next 5 years to this initiative.

Madame Chairman, Ranking Member Deutch, members of the subcommittee, I appreciate the opportunity to appear before you today and I look forward to answering any questions you might have. Thank you.

[The prepared statement of Mr. Roebuck follows:]

Testimony for the Record
William V. Roebuck
Deputy Assistant Secretary of State for Near Eastern Affairs
U.S. Department of State
Foreign Affairs Committee, Subcommittee on the Middle East and North Africa
U.S. House of Representatives
Hearing on *U.S. Policy Toward Morocco*
April 09, 2014

Chairman Ros-Lehtinen, Ranking Member Deutch, Members of the Subcommittee, I am honored to appear before you today to offer an overview of U.S. policy toward Morocco.

I am also pleased to appear before you today with USAID Deputy Assistant Administrator Alina Romanowski. I have had the pleasure of working closely with Ms. Romanowski to further our foreign policy objectives in Morocco and the region. We welcome the opportunity to speak to you today and look forward to answering any questions you may have regarding Morocco and our policy. [With your permission, I request that my full statement be submitted for the record.]

Bilateral Relationship

Madam Chairman, as you know, Morocco – the first nation to recognize the United States in 1777 – is an important and longstanding ally of the United States. We continue to enjoy a very strong bilateral relationship with Morocco, focused on promoting regional stability, supporting democratic reform efforts, countering violent extremism, and strengthening trade and cultural ties. Morocco – a major non-NATO ally since 2004 – is one of our closest counterterrorism partners in the region, and an active member of the Global Counterterrorism Forum. During its term on the UN Security Council, Morocco played an important role in international efforts to end the Syrian civil war. We also enjoy a strong economic relationship; our free trade agreement that entered into force in 2006 has increased bilateral trade by 254 percent.

We worked to strengthen this bilateral relationship during the November 2013 visit of King Mohammed VI to Washington. This provided an opportunity for the United States to reaffirm our close strategic partnership with Morocco and to discuss the best means of promoting security and prosperity in the region. In particular, we worked to deepen our consultations on regional issues, and stressed our shared priorities in Mali, Syria, the Maghreb, and the Sahel. We continued our conversations during the recent U.S.-Morocco Strategic Dialogue, which Secretary Kerry opened on April 4 in Rabat. The Dialogue, launched in 2012 out of a shared desire to find opportunities to strengthen the partnership between the United States and Morocco, discussed new avenues for cooperation in the political, security, economic, educational, and cultural spheres. We are also very pleased that our new Ambassador to Morocco, Dwight Bush, was confirmed in March and has arrived in Rabat.

Support for Democratic and Economic Reforms

Under King Mohammed VI, the Moroccan political system has gradually liberalized; the King founded the Arab world's first truth and reconciliation commission – to investigate abuses that occurred during his father's reign – and expanded women's rights. A new constitution was adopted in 2011, and Morocco's first Islamist-led government won nationwide democratic elections. However, much progress remains on implementing the guarantees and institutions, including increasing engagement of its citizens, under the new constitution. We have a robust dialogue with the Moroccan government on human rights and ways in which we can support the ongoing process of political reform.

We will continue to support Morocco as it undertakes these important reform efforts. Our bilateral assistance – roughly $31 million in FY 2013 – focuses on promoting economic, political, and social reforms; deepening our security partnership by supporting modern military and law enforcement agencies; promoting export control and antiterrorism as well as countering violent extremism efforts; developing a professional criminal justice system; and encouraging broad-based economic growth that provides expanded opportunities for women and youth. Our flagship assistance program has been Morocco's $698 million Millennium Challenge Corporation (MCC) compact, which closed in September 2013 and focused on agriculture, fisheries, and small enterprises. Morocco was reselected in December 2013 to develop a second MCC compact.

The United States supports Morocco's reform efforts, particularly the recent progress on military trials. In the Joint Statement issued on the occasion of the November 22 visit of King Mohammed VI to Washington, DC, President Obama welcomed the King's commitment to end the practice of military trials of civilians.

We are pleased to see this commitment made concrete in the Moroccan government's initiative to reform the Military Code of Justice and to exempt civilians from trial by military tribunals through a draft law which has moved to Parliament for approval. We have also remarked on the growing role of the National Council on Human Rights (CNDH) as a credible and proactive defender of human rights, and are encouraged by the Council of Government's decision to strengthen the CNDH by ensuring that government agencies address complaints directed to it. Both of these measures are important steps forward in strengthening the protection of human rights in Morocco and in realizing the promise of the 2011 Constitution.

Economic and Security Cooperation

There are many difficult challenges underlying the instability in the region today. The United States and Morocco are working together to address a number of those economic and security challenges, including addressing the issue of youth unemployment and youth discontent. Young people in Morocco make up approximately 30 percent of the country's population, and one tenth of the region's total youth population. Their levels of exclusion are high: 49 percent of Moroccan youth are neither in school, nor in the workforce, according to a recent World Bank survey. These young people are empowered by new communications technologies to see events across the world and to communicate with each other as never before. And some are frustrated by the lack of jobs and little economic opportunity.

Our mutual concern for peace and stability in the region means that the United States and Morocco are fully engaged in both economic and security cooperation. On economic cooperation, USAID's new Country Development Cooperation Strategy directly addresses the issue of youth unemployment through the creation of new vocational programs and career centers, to assist youth in finding jobs. The United States and Morocco also recently held the second U.S.-Morocco Business Development Conference in Rabat. Fifty-eight U.S. businesses participated in the conference in Morocco, resulting in increased business ties and helping advance our commercial and economic agenda to increase trade and investment.

In the area of security cooperation, Morocco is one of our closest counterterrorism (CT) partners in the Middle East and North Africa region. Instability in the region, porous borders, and the collapse of state institutions in northern Mali have increased regional threats and created new opportunities for cross border illicit flows and for violent extremist groups, such as al-Qaeda in the Islamic Maghreb

(AQIM), to gain ground and stage operations in both the Maghreb and the Sahel. However, due to Government of Morocco's broad, holistic, counterterrorism strategy of vigilant security measures, regional and international cooperation, socio-economic assistance, and counter-radicalization policies, it has been difficult for AQIM to effectively establish a foothold in Morocco.

The U.S. Department of Defense and Morocco held the eighth annual session of the U.S.-Morocco Defense Consultative Committee in December 2013. These meetings build on the already strong U.S.-Morocco security cooperation in the fields of training, exercise, and logistic support.

Morocco is also an active and constructive member of the Global Counterterrorism Forum and the Trans-Sahara Counterterrorism Partnership and has played a very positive role in the development and dissemination of best practices in combating terrorism, violent extremism, improving border security, and building capacity in the region. The United States looks to partner actively with Morocco to build its capacity to a point where it can aid its neighbors on many of these issues in the region.

Western Sahara

With regard to Western Sahara, the United States supports the United Nations-led process designed to bring about a peaceful, sustainable, and mutually-acceptable solution to the Western Sahara question. U.S. policy toward the Western Sahara has remained consistent for many years. We support the work of the UN Secretary-General's Personal Envoy for Western Sahara and UN-led efforts to find a peaceful, sustainable and mutually-agreed solution to the Western Sahara conflict. We urge the parties to work toward a resolution. With regard to the Moroccan autonomy plan we have made clear that Morocco's autonomy plan is serious, realistic, and credible, and that it represents a potential approach that could satisfy the aspirations of the people in the Western Sahara to run their own affairs in peace and dignity.

Educational and Cultural Cooperation

The United States and Morocco have a long history of people-to-people ties. Since 1967, our binational Fulbright program has been strengthening ties between our two countries. Fulbright Alumni have gone on to be government ministers, university presidents, eminent professors, and business leaders in Morocco. One recent example is Morocco's support of the J. Christopher Stevens Virtual Exchange Initiative, a public-private partnership between the Department of State, the J. Christopher Stevens Fund, the New Venture Fund, and the MacArthur Foundation to build innovative solutions that harness the power of virtual exchange platforms to address critical diplomatic challenges. The initiative is designed to fuel the largest ever growth in people-to-people exchanges between the United States and the broader Middle East, vastly increase the number and diversity of youth who have a meaningful cross-cultural experience, and catalyze the development and expansion of the field of virtual exchange globally. Morocco has graciously committed to donate $1 million per year over the next five years to this Initiative.

Another part of the United States and Morocco's long history of people-to-people ties is the Peace Corps. Morocco has one of the largest cadres of Peace Corps volunteers in the world and Peace Corps celebrated its 50th anniversary in Morocco last year. Historically, Peace Corps volunteers focused on a number of different areas; recently they have started to focus almost exclusively on the youth sector. As a direct result of the Arab spring turmoil, youth development has become a major focus for the Government of Morocco. As part of his new direction, King Mohammed VI has taken unprecedented steps to support programs that target education, life skills, illiteracy, and unemployment. Morocco anticipated the need for and requested an increase in the number of Peace Corps Volunteers serving youth in the country. With an already strong program working with youth, Peace Corps Morocco has re-focused its entire program to the youth sector and has excellent support from and collaboration with the Ministry of Youth and Sports.

Future Cooperation
As I mentioned at the outset, the United States and Morocco enjoy a very strong bilateral relationship, focused on promoting regional stability, supporting democratic reform efforts, countering violent extremism, and strengthening trade and cultural ties.

As part of this promotion of regional stability we will continue to work with Morocco on issues of peace and security and continue to foster greater economic growth. We are partnering with the Government of Morocco to focus on policies that will create jobs and growth, benefit the people, and knit the economy closer to the United States and the opportunities of the global economy. Progress in diplomatic agreements can help turn the extraordinary creativity and energy of people in this region toward the building of a better future – but it will take work, and we are working diligently with the Government of Morocco towards success.

Conclusion

Madam Chairman, Ranking Member Deutch, Members of the Subcommittee, I appreciate the opportunity to appear before you today, and I look forward to answering any questions you may have.

Ms. Ros-Lehtinen. Thank you very much, sir.

Ms. Romanowski.

STATEMENT OF MS. ALINA ROMANOWSKI, DEPUTY ASSISTANT ADMINISTRATOR, BUREAU FOR THE MIDDLE EAST, U.S. AGENCY FOR INTERNATIONAL DEVELOPMENT

Ms. Romanowski. Chairman Ros-Lehtinen, Ranking Member Deutch, members of the subcommittee, and Congressman Grimm, thank you for inviting me here today to discuss how USAID continues to support U.S. foreign policy and development objectives in Morocco. And I am very pleased to be here also with my colleague, Bill Roebuck, with whom I work closely every day.

For the past 56 years, we have partnered with the Government of Morocco to build a strong relationship that focuses on promoting economic growth, improving educational opportunities, and strengthening the effectiveness of civil society. During this time, we have worked to make substantial improvements in the lives of everyday Moroccans including improving maternal and child health, constructing two major dams, transforming thousands of semi-arid acres into productive agricultural land, and helping Morocco's microfinance sector.

We are proud and remain committed to this partnership which is why during the visit of King Mohammed VI to Washington last year, USAID and the Government of Morocco jointly launched a new 5-year country development strategy. Developed in collaboration with the Moroccan Government, civil society, and the private sector, the new strategy responds to the needs of Moroccan citizens and focuses on three key objectives, increasing youth employment, enhancing civic participation in governance, and improving education for children in primary schools. As we focus on these three objectives, we recognize that we must be strategic in our investments amid an increasingly strained budget outlook. Therefore, we are focusing like never before on strengthening alliances with key regional allies and building public-private partnerships with such entities as Microsoft, Volvo, and Chevron.

USAID's economic growth programs are aimed at directly addressing youth unemployment. Young people make up about 30 percent of Morocco's population. That is about 10 million people. Large numbers of Moroccan graduates are unable to find jobs commensurate with their education and training, while employers complain of skills, shortages, and mismatches. Without a trained workforce, capable of increasing productivity, Morocco cannot generate sufficient prosperity through private sector growth. To address this and other obstacles, USAID is launching the Youth Employability Project. This new initiative will facilitate partnerships between government ministries, Moroccan universities, and technical institutes, as well as local NGOs and the private sector to create workforce development services for a broad range of youth. For example, we are currently working with 40 startup Moroccan businesses to locate new markets and realize sustainable revenue flows.

In the Democracy and Governance sector, USAID is responding directly to the Government of Morocco's push to strengthen political parties and increase the roles of civil society organizations in the political process. We are currently working with more than 80 local governments to create platforms for dialogue between Moroccan citizens and their locally elected officials, especially for youth and women.

USAID's third strategic focus in Morocco is improving primary school education. USAID has improved quality and access to elementary and middle school, especially for rural girls. Enrollment of girls in rural areas increased from 62 percent in 2000 to 83 percent in 2004, but despite these gains, Morocco still faces an overall literacy rate of only 55 percent. In conjunction with Morocco's own education reform effort, USAID is targeting early grade reading. These programs are designed to improve early literacy and help curb primary grade dropout rates. USAID is also implementing innovative community and school-driven development projects in over 190 schools.

Finally, USAID is also responding to a critical challenge of countering violent extremism. In those programs, we target areas in Morocco where youth suffer from social, economic, and political disaffection and exclusion. These areas are known recruitment grounds for violent extremist and transnational terrorist networks. Our program is aimed at reintegrating at-risk youth into mainstream society, given Moroccan youth a voice, and opportunities in their communities.

So in conclusion, USAID is proud of the strong relationship we have built with the Government of Morocco over the past 56 years. Morocco continues to face significant challenges, but also significant opportunities. USAID programs will continue to provide assistance that will increase employment opportunities for Moroccan youth, build the reading skills of Moroccan children and advance participatory governance in addition to countering violent extremist threats and strengthening regional stability and security.

Thank you for the opportunity to appear before you today, and we are looking forward to answering your questions.

[The prepared statement of Ms. Romanowski follows:]

Statement of Alina L. Romanowski
Deputy Assistant Administrator, Bureau for the Middle East
U.S. Agency for International Development
U.S. House Committee on Foreign Affairs
Subcommittee on the Middle East and North Africa

"U.S. Policy Towards Morocco"

April 9, 2014

Chairman Ros-Lehtinen, Ranking Member Deutch, and Members of the Subcommittee: thank you for inviting me here today to discuss how the U.S. Agency for International Development (USAID) continues to support U.S. foreign policy objectives and national security interests in Morocco and the MENA region through our assistance. Thank you also for your continued support for our USAID Mission in Morocco. I am pleased to be here with my colleague, Bill Roebuck, with whom I work closely every day.

Introduction

When our Administrator, Rajiv Shah, testified before you earlier today, he talked about USAID's mission around the world—partnering to end extreme poverty and to promote resilient, democratic societies while advancing our security and prosperity. This mission is one that USAID has embodied in Morocco, one of our oldest Missions, since 1958.

For the past 56 years, we have partnered with the Government of Morocco to build a strong bilateral relationship that focuses on promoting economic growth, improving educational opportunities and strengthening the effectiveness of civil society's political engagement. During this time, we have also worked together to make substantial improvements in the lives of everyday Moroccan citizens, including significantly improving maternal and child health, constructing two major dams, transforming thousands of semi-arid acres into productive agricultural use, and developing the microfinance sector in Morocco through high profile credit guarantees. We are proud and remain committed to this partnership, which is why in 2013, USAID and the Government of Morocco completed a new five-year Country Development Cooperation Strategy, or CDCS, that affirms this commitment.

During last year's visit of King Mohammed VI to Washington, DC, we jointly launched USAID's CDCS and reaffirmed our long history of cooperation and collaboration. The CDCS is a strategic plan developed in collaboration with the Moroccan Government, civil society, and the private sector designed to create a prosperous future for the Moroccan people. The strategy responds to the needs of Moroccan citizens and focuses on three key objectives. First, we want to increase youth employment, a challenge across the region. Second, we want to enhance civic participation in governance; and, third, we want to increase access to and improve the quality of education for children in primary schools.

As we focus on these three objectives, we recognize that we must be strategic in our investments amid an increasingly strained budget outlook. Therefore, we are focusing like never before on strengthening alliances with key regional allies and building public-private partnerships including Microsoft, Volvo, and Chevron. Partnerships with the private sector and regional allies promote stability and economic growth.

Increasing Youth Employment while promoting Economic Growth and Job Creation

USAID's economic growth programs are aimed at directly addressing the issue of youth unemployment. Morocco is in a paradoxical situation: large numbers of graduates are unable to find jobs commensurate with their education and training, while employers complain of skills shortages and mismatches. Young people make up approximately 30 percent of Morocco's population — about 10 million people. Youth unemployment rates estimated at approximately 28 percent have historically resulted in serious social and political tensions. Moreover, without a trained workforce capable of increasing productivity, Morocco cannot generate sufficient shared prosperity through private sector growth. This cadre of unemployed youth with education degrees of 9th grade or above is best positioned to drive the desired structural transformation of the Moroccan economy. The disproportionately high rate of unemployment among secondary and post-secondary graduates is linked to labor-force and education-system factors in addition to the challenging job growth situation. The absence of career services and the lack of integration of work preparedness in the curricula of Moroccan universities and vocational schools exacerbate the situation.

To address this and other obstacles, USAID/Morocco is preparing to launch a new initiative, the USAID Youth Employability Project, to improve the employability of university and vocational school students by increasing access to and improving the quality of career services. Through this initiative, USAID will facilitate partnerships between government ministries, Moroccan universities and technical institutes, as well as local NGOs and the private sector to develop demand-driven workforce development services that reach a broad range of youth. An example of this type of programming is our current work with 40 start-up and growth stage Moroccan businesses, helping them locate new markets and realize sustainable flows of revenue. This program recently awarded its first grant to the American Chamber of Commerce to develop an Export Lab for Moroccan businesses interested in breaking into the American market. They have also begun to facilitate preparations for the annual Global Entrepreneurship Summit, which will be held in Morocco in the fall 2014.

Increasing Civic Participation in Governance by Supporting Democratic Institutions and Promoting Civil Society

Morocco's new constitutional requirements have created an incentive for more inclusive governance, and civil society and political parties are now constitutionally empowered to participate in governance. USAID's democracy and governance programs respond directly to the Government of Morocco's push to strengthen political parties and increase the roles of civil society organizations enabling Morocco to implement its reform agenda in a peaceful and sustainable way. The USAID mission is currently working with more than 80 local governments, known in Morocco as communes, and creating platforms for dialogue between Moroccan citizens and their locally elected officials, especially for youth and women. USAID's engagement in this sector includes training that encourages increased transparency and accountability by officials and opportunities for enhanced responsiveness to citizens' demands as well as women's leadership roles. For example, USAID's leadership training helped a female parliamentarian in the province of Fez to develop greater expertise in local governance. Over the past two years, this parliamentarian has become involved in the creation of a network of locally elected women officials who promote collaboration and knowledge sharing among women. These women hope to bring together three existing local networks to further unify their advocacy efforts into a regional network that promotes women's participation in local governance.

Moroccan citizens have long been detached from their political parties due to a lack of clear policy, vision or consideration for citizen involvement, particularly of women and youth. USAID will help Moroccan political parties be more responsive to the needs of their constituents and increase the involvement of youth and women in politics. In fact, since USAID started working to strengthen political parties in Morocco, the percentage of women in Parliament has increased from less than 1 percent to over 12 percent. Moving forward, technical assistance will be provided in the effective use of public opinion to inform policy agendas, the development of youth and women's branches of political parties at the national and grassroots levels, and the development of individual plans to strengthen internal party capacity. In addition to increasing the role of women and youth in the political process, USAID will also support electoral reform initiatives.

In addition to working with political parties and on elections, USAID is also focusing on strengthening Moroccan civil society organizations (CSOs), that have the potential to contribute more effectively to public policy processes and inclusive governance in Morocco. Through its democracy and governance programs, USAID will assist Moroccan CSOs in oversight efforts and capacity development. We will also help them develop their own constituencies and memberships and to use information and communications technologies. By increasing the capacity of civil society to engage the government on behalf of its citizens and facilitating the development of institutionalized mechanisms for civic participation in government decision-making, Morocco will be better situated to implement its reform agenda in a peaceful and sustainable fashion.

Improving Educational Achievements of Moroccan Youth

The third pillar of USAID's new strategic focus in Morocco is on improving educational attainment for primary school students. USAID has helped improve access to school, especially for girls in rural areas, and strengthen school quality and performance at the elementary and middle school levels. Enrollment of girls in rural areas increased from 62 percent in 2000 to 83 percent in 2004. In target zones, girls' enrollment increased by 24 percent in 6th grade, and community support for girls education expanded. Between 2009 and 2013, the dropout rate decreased in target regions from over 15 percent to around 8 percent. Despite these gains, Morocco still faces key education challenges, including an overall literacy rate of only 55 percent.

Moving forward, in conjunction with Morocco's own education reform effort, USAID will promote higher levels of educational attainment by targeting early grade reading. Poor reading skills increase children's chances that they will fall behind in school, setting the stage for future dropout. These early grade reading programs are designed to improve early literacy and help curb primary grade dropout rates. Classroom-based assessment and monitoring of student progress will also be an important component of USAID support. Community-based reading initiatives that support school retention will reinforce in-school learning and facilitate re-enrollment for primary grade dropouts.

USAID is now implementing innovative, completely community and school-driven development projects in over 190 schools. These projects are not based on infrastructure needs but are specifically directed to improve learning. Examples include library materials, extra-curricular programming for students, and remedial learning support. Initiatives to prevent school dropout in high-risk areas are implemented through coordination with civil society organizations and community- and parent-based groups. As a result of our life skills and employability programs for use in after-school clubs in middle schools, 670 teachers were trained through student clubs established in 191 schools, reaching 10,400 students.

USAID has been applying innovative approaches and has been using technology and partnership to promote educational solutions in Morocco. For example, in partnership with the U.S. National Academy of Sciences, L'Ecole Nationale de l'Industrie Minérale (ENIM) and the U.S. private sector firm Institute for Disabilities Research and Training, Inc. (IDRT), we supported the development of an important technology that will facilitate access to information to a large portion of Morocco's hearing impaired population. The technology provides real-time translation between Moroccan Sign Language and standard written Arabic, which will have a significant impact on the education, health, and welfare of Morocco's hearing impaired. In addition to developing this new technology, this partnership is working with linguists to further develop the vocabulary in Moroccan Sign Language.

Countering Violent Extremism

USAID is also responding to a critical fourth challenge we face in Morocco, that of countering violent extremist threats. Countering violent extremist threats in Morocco and in the region is a crucial element of both regional and U.S. national security interests. While the incidence of violent extremism in Morocco is currently low, several incidents have occurred in Morocco over the past decade that should not be ignored, and societal factors such as social exclusion or lack of economic opportunities increase that risk. Morocco has developed a nuanced approach to countering violent extremism that seeks to engage and include at-risk populations. In support of this effort, USAID programs work with at-risk youth to engage in the political process and increase economic opportunities. The program also strengthens the capacity of government and non-government institutions to improve the quality of services provided to the targeted youth group, thereby helping to ensure long-term sustainability.

In our countering violent extremism programming, we target areas of Morocco where youth suffer from social, economic and political disaffection and exclusion – often evidenced by high rates of illiteracy, school dropout, and unemployment. These areas are known recruitment grounds for violent extremist and transnational terrorist networks. To reintegrate at-risk youth into mainstream society, we support programming that gives youth a voice and opportunities in their communities. Our programming works at the neighborhood level, with neighborhood associations, government and the youth themselves to provide a range of support: from non-formal education and vocational training, the provision of basic social services, career counseling and job placement, to advocacy training. Capacity building for public and private social service providers targeting at-risk youth will increase sustainability and expand the reach of program activities, currently focused on at-risk youth in northern Morocco, specifically in the cities of Tetouan and Tangier.

Conclusion

USAID is proud of the strong relationship we have built with the Government of Morocco over the past 56 years. Morocco continues to face significant challenges, but also significant opportunities. USAID programs will continue to provide assistance that will increase employment opportunities for Moroccan youth, build the early reading skills of Moroccan children, and advance participatory governance, in addition to countering violent extremist threats and strengthening regional stability and security.

Thank you for the opportunity to appear before you today, and I look forward to answering your questions.

Ms. ROS-LEHTINEN. Thank you. And thank you to both of you for excellent testimony. We will begin our question and answer period.

As we have said, the U.S. and Morocco share a strategic and dynamic bilateral relationship. In the omnibus bill that we passed in January, Congress authorized that funds designated for Morocco could also be used in the Western Sahara for literacy training programs. The bill requests that a report from the State Department on this issue and the report is due next week. Can you describe what the report will entail and if it will be delivered on time?

Then on the threat of fundamentalism in the area, the threat of radical Islam and extremism spreading through North Africa and indeed throughout the entire African continent is a very real threat and a cause for alarm. That is why the United States has put such an emphasis on working with Morocco to counter these threats.

How would you describe the cooperation with Morocco on the counterterrorism front? Is it as good as it can be? Is it getting better? Are you satisfied with it? And to what extent are programs like the Trans-Sahara Counterterrorism Program working? What more needs to be done both on Morocco's side and the U.S. side to improve it?

And as we discussed just last week, Secretary Kerry was in Rabat to take part in the second round of the U.S.-Morocco Strategic Dialogue. Can you briefly explain what came out of that latest round in the dialogue? What did we achieve? What did we accomplish? And what challenges still remain? Thank you.

Mr. ROEBUCK. Thank you, Madame Chairwoman. I will start maybe in reverse order and work my way back up. The Strategic Dialogue was a big success. Secretary Kerry opened it. We had a strong team that came out from the State Department that participated in it. The purpose of this dialogue is to accentuate and highlight the strong strategic partnership we have with Morocco and we focus on a range of areas, three working groups in particular: Political security, economic and commercial cooperation, and education and cultural cooperation. I think we made strong steps forward in all three of these groups. The political and security group, there was a robust discussion of Morocco's progress on domestic reforms and also encouragement from Morocco's efforts on counterterrorism. The economic and commercial cooperation group discussed promoting regional economic integration and also Morocco and the U.S. trade investment relationship and particularly trying to strengthen the benefits for Morocco of the U.S.-Morocco free trade agreement.

On education and cultural cooperation, as I mentioned earlier, there was a discussion of the Chris Stevens Virtual Exchange Initiative, efforts to improve on interfaith dialogue and understanding, and a discussion of various educational and cultural exchange programs we have with Morocco, including for example, the Fulbright program.

On the threat of fundamentalism and extremism in Morocco and in the region at large, I share your concern, Madame Chairman. This is not a new phenomenon. This is something that has been developing in the region over the past decade really. It has been fed in some ways in the past several years by developments in Mali, in the wider Sahel, and also in Libya where there has been a deteriorating security situation in the past 2½ years. We work very closely with Morocco on counterterrorism. I think that our partnership is quite strong. We have a number of programs, a number of vehicles that we use to fund these programs. Trans-Saharan Counterterrorism Partnership is one. We use funding through NADR as well as INL money to—it is focused primarily on strengthening Morocco's law enforcement and criminal justice system. It also provides training for law enforcement people who are involved in antiterrorism efforts to strengthen their professionalism and strengthen their efforts with things like Internet, forensic investigation, the ability to do criminal investigations in general and use these types of law enforcement tools as a means for combatting terrorism.

Ms. ROS-LEHTINEN. Thank you very much. And I apologize, my time is up. Thank you very much.

Mr. Deutch is recognized.

Mr. DEUTCH. Thank you, Madame Chairman. Deputy Assistant Secretary Roebuck, just to follow up on this discussion, clearly, security cooperation is a critical component of the relationship. And you had included in your testimony the figure of 49 percent of Moroccan youth are neither in school nor in the workforce which is a staggering figure, I think. I know we share concerns with Morocco that some segments of that population might be vulnerable to extremist recruitment. The porous borders of North Africa make it easy to say, go be paid to fight in Syria for a few months, come back to Morocco. Can you discuss ways in which the U.S. and Morocco are working together to address that specific security concern?

Mr. ROEBUCK. The issue of foreign fighters?

Mr. DEUTCH. Yes.

Mr. ROEBUCK. The United States and Morocco work closely on this. This is largely an effort that has to be directed by Morocco, but we consult with the Moroccan Government closely on this issue. We recognize that it is a serious issue for the Morocco Government. A lot of it has to do with the need for a multi-faceted approach to this and to a counterterrorism approach in general and this is what the Moroccan Government has in place. Part of their focus is I would call it vigilant security efforts or operational efforts. Part of it is side efforts through countering violent extremism with education. Part of it is focused on education and socio-economic assistance.

I think Morocco has a broad, focused counterterrorism policy and that is what they use to address this particular issue that you focused on which is foreign fighters going to Syria and coming back. I can give you more detail if you would like it, but that is the general approach that they use and we are very supportive of it.

Mr. DEUTCH. I appreciate that. Ms. Romanowski, I was pleased to see USAID placing such great emphasis in the new country development cooperation strategy on youth unemployment which was mentioned earlier was around 30 percent. We know the major cause of the unrest in 2011 came from disaffected youth. Morocco recently announced ambitious plans to build up industry and create ½ million new sustainable jobs by 2020 and to significantly increase the share of industry in GDP to 23 percent versus the 14 percent today.

How will USAID's programs work in concert with this new initiative and are we going to have to realign some of our programming in light of that effort?

Ms. ROMANOWSKI. Thank you for the question, sir. I think we have already realigned our programs in a sense through the conversation, the dialogue we have had with the Government of Morocco when we built this new 5-year development strategy. And specifically in our economic program, the Employability, we are focusing on bringing universities and vocational school students and the private sector and the government to find ways that we can improve employment skills of these young people and then offer them actual centers where they can do that and also where the private sector can come together. So this conversation, this particular program that we are focusing on is doing exactly that. And it is not out of sync with, I think, supporting what their efforts are trying to do in attracting more investment.

Mr. DEUTCH. Great. And finally, another focus of USAID is increasing civic participation, particularly for women and as part of a series of electoral reforms, Parliament now has a 66 quota for women. I would like for you to just talk about the trend lines that you are seeing among women in politics, how do we get there, how do meet those goals?

Ms. ROMANOWSKI. I think the trend lines in Moroccan politics for women are positive. In the last two visits or three visits I have been to Morocco, I have met many of the women parliamentarians and politicians and those who are active in politics, both at the local level and at the national level and both through our programs, the local governance program and also through our political party strengthening. We are making sure that not just women, but also young women and young men are part of reaching out and getting a more active participation. So in the many years I have been working in Morocco in this area, I see that there is a lot of interest in women to come into politics, which is always a good thing.

Mr. DEUTCH. Great. Thank you. Thank you, Madame Chairman.

Ms. ROS-LEHTINEN. Thank you, Mr. Deutch. Subcommittee Chair Chabot is recognized.

Mr. CHABOT. Thank you, Madame Chair. Morocco has been supportive of the Arab-Israeli peace negotiations. And recently an anti-Israel group, the Moroccan Observatory Against Normalization, an organization that is working to end commerce and international ties between Israel and Morocco, published a list of people and institutions it accuses of collaboration with the Jewish state. How has King Mohammed and the Moroccan Government responded to this? Is this group a cause for concern that could negatively affect Moroccan-Israeli relations? And what steps can the administration take or has it taken to ensure that productive relations between Israel and Morocco continue?

Mr. ROEBUCK. Thank you, Congressman Chabot. Morocco and Israel have a long history of positive relations. With regard to these developments that you have pointed to, our review is that these efforts have stalled and they are likely to—we think they will stay stalled. We believe that the values in Morocco of religious interfaith dialogue and religious tolerance will triumph. We know that there have been efforts to move a piece of legislation which is similar to what you are referring to. That effort has stalled. I believe that King Mohammed IV and the Government of Morocco have worked very hard to foster an atmosphere of religious tolerance and interfaith understanding that will prevent such measures from moving forward.

Mr. CHABOT. Thank you. We know there are a lot of bad actors in the region and that Moroccan authorities have taken a proactive approach to countering the presence of extremists ideologies in the country. Could either of you comment on some of the successful elements of their counterterrorism programs?

Mr. ROEBUCK. I will start, Congressman Chabot and Alina, if you would like to say something, you are welcome to.

As we mentioned earlier in my testimony, the Moroccans have been very effective counterterrorism partners. The reason that they have been effective is that they developed a strategy that has several different elements to it, all of which are proven elements that are effective in countering terrorism. It is not just operational, although that is a piece of it. The Moroccan Government has also been very good at developing programs designed to counter balance extremism. It builds off of the Moroccan Government effort and the King's effort to promote a tolerant, moderate brand of Islam in the kingdom. They have made efforts to train imams, religious leaders, from neighboring countries in ways that would encourage political moderation and religious moderation including a large number of imams from nearby Mali where there have been a lot of problems with these extremists.

So the bottom line is that they have been very effective because they have used tools in the tool kit. In addition, they have been very active as regional international partners, cooperating on counterterrorism, both with our efforts on the Global Counterterrorism Forum and the Trans-Saharan Counterterrorism Partnership and working with their neighbors, they posted a border conference for Libya and they have done other things on foreign fighters working with The Netherlands. So across a wide range of fronts, they have taken action on all of them. That is why they have been effective. Thank you, sir.

Mr. CHABOT. Thank you, sir. Ms. Romanowski.

Ms. ROMANOWSKI. I would point in addition to our broader workforce development program for young people, I would point to two other programs. One is our civic participation program that focuses on marginalized urban youth where we are working with the local governance structures and elected officials to better focus on being responsive to the concerns of young people, particularly marginalized youth in their areas.

And then the second one which is very specific to two areas where I think we and the Government of Morocco have identified as being particularly regions of struggle and that is in the neighborhood of Tangier and Tetouan where we have focused a youth program that responds to those specific neighborhoods in trying to again bring out the voices and make the marginalized youth much more confident that they can be a participatory and a constructive voice even in their local neighborhoods.

Mr. CHABOT. Thank you. In the time that I have remaining, I would like to turn briefly to trade. Some argue that the U.S.-Moroccan trade agreement limits stronger economic integration between Morocco and other African nations. Would you agree with that? And do you believe that the U.S. and Morocco, that both countries have mutually benefitted from our trade partnership? And what does the future of U.S.-Moroccan trade relations look like, in 17 seconds.

Mr. ROEBUCK. Thank you, Congressman. I think the free trade agreement has been a huge benefit for both sides. The United States has benefitted somewhat more in the initial years than the Moroccans, but both sides have seen huge increases in bilateral trade. I do not believe that it has been a hindrance to Moroccan trade with the region and I think they have a huge, bright future trading with us and with other partners. They are a hub for Europe, but also for Africa and we are working with them to strengthen the ways in which they can benefit from our free trade agreement. Thank you.

Mr. CHABOT. Well done. You took 41 seconds, but well done.

Ms. ROS-LEHTINEN. Very good. Thank you. I am looking forward to reading your article Bloomsday in Baghdad, Reading Joys in Iraq. I am going to look that up.

Ms. Frankel.

Ms. FRANKEL. Thank you, Madame Chair. And a number of my questions were answered. Thank you. First, I want to follow up on Mr. Deutch's question about women. I understand that 3 years ago when Morocco adopted a new constitution it guaranteed gender equality. However, I am told that there is still not the equality the women would like. For example, I think the legal marriage age was raised from 15 to 18, but a judge can still grant and do grant permission for marriages at a much younger age and also that there are inheritance laws that still favor men. I don't know, those are just a couple of examples. But I wanted to know what your opinion is on the status of women in Morocco.

Thank you for sharing with us some of the programs that USAID and others are putting into effect, I guess to counter a possible Arab Spring and to minimize terrorism. I want to know whether there are any measures of effectiveness, any measures to see whether or not any of these programs are being effective.

And last question is and this is also a followup, if you could say a little bit more as to the strategic importance of Morocco, explaining why we are putting these efforts into Morocco and their relationship to their neighboring African countries.

Mr. ROEBUCK. Thank you. Thank you, Congresswoman. On the issue of reform in women's position in society, I would say that it is a work in progress in Morocco with regard to reform for women's rights and reform writ large. The Moroccans embarked on a major reform in 2003 and 2004 that benefitted women, the reform of their family code. It strengthened provisions relating to inheritance, divorce, child custody and similar type provisions. The 2011 constitution strengthened further some of those reforms and made constitutionally clear the equality between men and women. But some of the issues that you raise, child marriage, the low age for women that can be married remain a problem and I think the Moroccan Government is aware of it, but our sense is that they are reform oriented. They want to make improvements. They are continuing to do this and what we have seen in the last decade really is a steady move of progress.

One of the human rights people who went out in 2012, noted an emerging culture of human rights in Morocco. For example, it is just another example of the type of reform that has been available to witness out there.

Just a word on the strategic importance of Morocco in the region and Alina, I will let you say something if you would like to on the effectiveness of our programs. We have a strategic relationship with Morocco because it is such an important country in the region. Its geographic location is very important. It is involved in one of the major conflict areas, the Western Sahara, which is important and is creating some issues with Algeria. Morocco is a key country for us in helping to counter violent extremism. It is a critical partner in that and it is a critical trade partner. And it is a critical country as a voice of moderate Islam. For all those reasons, it is a very important strategic partner for the United States. Thank you, ma'am.

Ms. ROMANOWSKI. On the issue of measuring effectiveness and our monitoring evaluation, we do monitor and evaluate our programs and in fact, the opportunity to do a new 5-year country strategy afforded us that opportunity to go back and review the programs that we were working and where we felt they needed to really shift and keep up with what the changes that were going on in Morocco. That is what caused us really to redo the economic growth piece to focus on the workforce development.

On our political and democracy and governance programs, we realized we needed to continue to strengthen those institutions that are part of that political process, like political parties, strengthen the local governance and work specifically again to continue to support the engagement of young people as well as women in politics and in the political process. We do continue and will continue to strongly monitor our program.

Ms. FRANKEL. Thank you, Madame Chair.

Ms. ROS-LEHTINEN. Thank you, Ms. Frankel. And I thank Mr. Weber for being nice enough to allow me jump him in turn because Mr. Grimm needs to get back to his subcommittee.

So Mr. Grimm is recognized for 5 minutes. Thank you for visiting us.

Mr. GRIMM. Thank you for having me, Chairman. Thank you, Mr. Weber. I appreciate the courtesy. Thank you to the witnesses.

I would like to step back for a second and just expand a little bit. The chairwoman mentioned before about the report, obviously, in the omnibus in January Congress authorized the funds designated for Morocco. It could also be used for the Western Sahara Literacy Training Program and my understanding is that that report is due to Congress next week, Mr. Roebuck. As far you know, is it on schedule to be delivered next week?

Mr. ROEBUCK. Yes, sir. We are preparing the report and it will be delivered in compliance with the law.

Mr. GRIMM. Is there any way you can thumbnail, obviously, I am not looking for details, but just give me some idea of what to expect, any highlights of what we can expect to see in that report?

Mr. ROEBUCK. I think the report will describe our efforts to provide assistance to Morocco and it will outline some of the areas where we have provided that assistance addressing the particular areas that the legislation wants to see more information on. And it will make the point with regard to assistance for Morocco that would be used in the Western Sahara, the United States, our policy is that we should not take any actions that would be perceived as undermining our support for the U.N.-led mediation process and that is a pillar of our policy. And the report would include that point.

Mr. GRIMM. Thank you. I appreciate that. Changing gears a little bit, as a member that represents New York City, financial services industry is an area of great interest to me, so I am very happy to see that Morocco is becoming a destination for many U.S. companies, not just as an export market, but also as a platform for exports into Africa, Europe, and broader Middle East. The new Casablanca finance city project is poised to become I think one of the central economic hubs for international companies that are looking or are already doing business throughout the African continent.

Is there anything that you can tell us about how American companies are using Morocco both as an export market, but also as a gateway to the entire region?

Mr. ROEBUCK. Thank you, Congressman. I would say just in short that the primary way that American companies so far are working in Morocco is to use the huge vehicle of the free trade agreement which has been in place and entered into force in 2006 which gives U.S. companies an ability to invest in Morocco and to export there. It also, in turn, gives Morocco the opportunity to do the same here. I think that is the big benefit and that is where we are focusing. We have also recently signed when King Mohammed VI was here a trade facilitation agreement which will further shore up those efforts. Thank you.

Mr. GRIMM. Ms. Romanowski, anything you would like to add?

Ms. ROMANOWSKI. In my most recent conversations with Moroccan businessman, and that was Friday night while I was there for the strategic dialogue, it was very clear that they were looking to some of our programs to be able to help them build a stronger network with American companies and they were very conscious of the fact that American companies were coming into Morocco. So I think that they were looking forward to it and I think the trend is very positive.

Mr. GRIMM. Great. Thank you, again. I am going to yield back the rest of my time.

Ms. ROS-LEHTINEN. Thank you very much.

Mr. GRIMM. Thank you, Madame Chairwoman.

Ms. ROS-LEHTINEN. Thanks for joining us and thanks for your leadership with the Moroccan caucus.

And now I am thrilled—we will recognize, Mr. Connolly, I am sorry——

Mr. CONNOLLY. No, no, thrilled, keep going.

Ms. ROS-LEHTINEN. What a thrill it is to recognize Mr. Connolly of Virginia for his question and answer period.

Mr. CONNOLLY. Thank you, Madame Chairman. A welcome to the panel. Let me ask Mr. Roebuck what has been the impact of the repression and military crackdown in Egypt on both the Moroccan Government and to the extent we know it, public opinion of Morocco?

Mr. ROEBUCK. Thank you, sir. For the question. It is probably—it might be a little difficult for me to assess that directly, but I will say based on my read of the region in general, people in the region have looked very closely at what has happened in Egypt. They have taken note. I think, for example, in Tunisia, some of the political parties watched very carefully what happened in Egypt. It probably made them more flexible maybe in the types of national dialogue talks that they were having and helped lead to a breakthrough with a new government and a new constitution.

Morocco was in a little different situation. It didn't have elections approaching in the fall when a lot of this was going on. I suspect the people in Morocco are concerned about what is going on in Egypt and they are looking at it very carefully. It may be causing them to reevaluate some of their conceptions about the Arab Spring and about democratic evolution and how fast it can happen and how some of the possible side effects of that type of turmoil. But a lot of those effects, at least in Morocco, are not as visible as they might be in some of the other countries in North Africa. I took a stab at answering your question. Thank you, sir.

Mr. CONNOLLY. I think it behooves us to sort of look at that question because hopefully Morocco and the Moroccan Government and the Moroccan people look at that and go, that is not where we want to go for lots of different reasons with lots of different dynamics, but let me ask you about—where is the Polisario right now? What is their political standing? What is their appeal? What influence, if any, do they have in the western part of the country?

Mr. ROEBUCK. The Polisario is a long-standing political organization that represents residents of Western Sahara who have advocated for independence.

Ms. ROS-LEHTINEN. If you could speak a little bit closer to the microphone.

Mr. CONNOLLY. You need to speak closer to the mic, Mr. Roebuck.

Ms. ROS-LEHTINEN. It is hard to hear.

Mr. ROEBUCK. Sorry.

Mr. CONNOLLY. And Madame Chairman if I could have that 1 minute and 50 seconds back.

Mr. ROEBUCK. The Polisario is the political organization that advocates for independence and for a referendum in Western Sahara. I think their influence is somewhat circumscribed in the last decade. I think——

Mr. CONNOLLY. Well, all right, Mr. Roebuck. I am old enough to remember when the Spanish gave it us.

Mr. ROEBUCK. Right.

Mr. CONNOLLY. And I am old enough to remember when Polisario emerged as a political force of some sort.

Mr. ROEBUCK. Right.

Mr. CONNOLLY. What we are trying to get at here is are they stronger? Are they weaker? Are their tentacles growing? Are they retreating? Are they actually kind of a fringe force at this point? Has the Moroccan Government been able to exercise sovereignty in a meaningful and real way that is recognized and respected by the people who live in the western part of the country or what?

Mr. ROEBUCK. Thank you, Congressman. It is a conflict that is an area that remains sort of conflict. You know, there are two parties to it. The United States' view is that those parties have to reach a mutually agreed upon solution. In answer to your question about are they weaker or are they stronger, I think probably over the past decade or so, they have gotten weaker, I am not sure politically. I am just speculating there. But they remain a key party in that conflict and our view is that the parties have to reach a solution and it can't be one that is imposed. So weaker or not, they remain a party to the conflict and we support a process that would be a U.N.-lead negotiations process between them and the Moroccan Government.

In terms of sovereignty, the territory of Western Sahara is considered by the U.N. as a non-self governing territory. Morocco exercises a non-official, sort of an administrator for its part of the territory, but it is not recognized by the U.N. as an official administering power for the Western Sahara. The key point for us is that this has got to be done through a negotiated process.

Mr. CONNOLLY. Just one more question if I may, Madame Chairman. Does anybody think Western Sahara could actually function as an independent sovereign state viably?

Mr. ROEBUCK. It is a difficult question to answer. I think in terms of explaining our policy, we don't sort of reach that level of inquiry. We prefer to focus on a process that lets the parties reach a solution, rather than looking at the situation and saying well, this side of the conflict doesn't have a viable solution to it, if you see what I am saying.

Mr. CONNOLLY. Not really. I mean what is so hard about the United States Government deciding in our humble opinion Country X could never stand alone as a sovereign state viably? Why can't we make that decision from time to time? We don't have to.

Mr. ROEBUCK. Right. I suppose we could, but we haven't reached that decision.

Mr. CONNOLLY. We have not reached that decision.

Mr. ROEBUCK. No. Our policy is not based on that type of conclusion. It is based on a process where the parties who are involved in a conflict have to reach a negotiated settlement.

Mr. CONNOLLY. Does the Moroccan Government agree with that position?

Mr. ROEBUCK. You might want to ask Ambassador Bouhlal who is here. I think the Moroccans have put forward a proposal which is autonomy under Moroccan sovereignty as their solution to that conflict. We believe that is a serious, realistic, and credible proposal. It is a potential approach to address the concerns of the people of Western Sahara and help them to live their lives in justice and dignity. So we think it is a potential approach. But in the end, we don't believe you can impose it.

Mr. CONNOLLY. Of course. Thank you. My time is up.

Ms. ROS-LEHTINEN. Thank you, Mr. Connolly. Mr. Weber. Thank you for your patience. Thank you.

Mr. WEBER. Thank you. Gosh, so many questions. Morocco receives substantial U.S. development aid in bilateral trade investment and that has increased following a 2006 free trade agreement. Our trade partnership with Morocco has increased following 2006 free trade agreement. How much?

Mr. ROEBUCK. Our trade has increased about 400 percent.

Mr. WEBER. Would you put in that in dollars?

Mr. ROEBUCK. I am not sure I have the dollar value, but it is a big increase on both sides. It has increased about 400 percent for the United States and between 150 and 200 percent on the Moroccan side. So it has been a big benefit for both, but a bigger benefit so far for U.S. exports and we are working with the Moroccans through our commercial law development program, through USAID, through the Millennium Challenge Corporation to even that out with some competitiveness efforts so that Moroccans can equally benefit from that.

Mr. WEBER. I saw that Morocco recently concluded a 5-year $697.5 million MCC compact which focused on alleviating poverty and all these goals. Successful?

Mr. ROEBUCK. I think it was very successful. Our assessment, it focused on sustainable tourism, sustainable fisheries and agriculture. It educated with basic literacy about 40,000 relatively poor people who were involved in those three fields. Eighty percent of those people were women. It helped build a tourist infrastructure in Fez Medina and also focused a little bit to a certain degree on financial services in a few other areas.

Morocco was recently reselected for a second compact. I think many people were impressed with the way it engaged on this Millennium Challenge Corporation with its institutions and its sort of enthusiasm. And we are moving forward with shaping a second compact for Morocco.

Mr. WEBER. I saw that and then my further reading it said that the bicameral legislature consisted of chamber of counselors who are indirectly elected and a chamber of reps who are directly elected. Explain that to me.

Mr. ROEBUCK. The chamber that is directly elected, that is the parliamentary elections that took place in 2011.

Mr. WEBER. Was it like the senators in our original constitution? They were elected by the states, similar?

Mr. ROEBUCK. It is a similar election. They indirectly elected people, it is more of an appointment, basically. A lot of them are appointed.

Mr. WEBER. Okay. And I noticed that I think one of my colleagues over on the other side alluded to the women's, the improvement of women's socio-economic rise was the 2004 revision of the Family Code that aimed to improve women's socio-economic rights. Has that been successful? Can you give me a status update or Ms. Romanowski, is that your bailiwick?

Ms. ROMANOWSKI. Well, actually, I think it is everyone's bailiwick.

Mr. WEBER. Okay.

Ms. ROMANOWSKI. Of engaging Moroccans and supporting Moroccan women and their rights. And through our programs we ensure that all of the USAID programs make sure that women are included and supported and specifically when it comes to our democracy and governance, we are making sure that women who want to be, who get into politics have the kind of training and skills and have the advantage and also in our economic workforce development project.

Mr. WEBER. So you all feel that it has been successful?

Ms. ROMANOWSKI. Yes. There is a lot more work to do. That is true across the region. But I think Morocco actually stands out as making some——

Mr. WEBER. Let me move on. I am running out of time here. Further my reading, it says that in talking about the division between Western Sahara and Morocco, that there were some who were concerned that Western Sahara would actually become a training ground for terrorists and that they were concerned about those coming back from Iraq and even that—some of those Western Sahara potential terrorists had been trained in Western Europe? Is that right? Are you aware of that, Mr. Roebuck?

Mr. ROEBUCK. Thank you, Congressman, for that question. I am not aware of that report. Our general assessment of the Western Sahara is as follows. It is a large space. We don't think that it is good for a space that big to be an ungoverned space. That is why we support the U.N. being there with the MINURSO organization. But in terms of what you are talking about which is some sort of ties between terrorists and the people in the Western Sahara, to our knowledge, we are not aware of significant terrorist activity in the Western Sahara and we are not aware of links between, for example, the Polisario, and terrorist organizations like the ones you have cited.

Mr. WEBER. And then one final question, if I may, Madame Chair. In talks about recent congressional actions, Morocco and the Polisario have advocates on both sides, directly appeal to Congress to support their positions on the Western Sahara. Many Members of Congress support Morocco's position asserting sovereignty over the territory. So I don't mean to put you on the spot, but how many Members of Congress support that position, do you know?

Mr. ROEBUCK. I do not, sir. I don't know exactly what the numbers would be. As I mentioned to Congressman Connolly, I mean our review is the issue of sovereignty is something that should be resolved through negotiations with the parties, but both sides have put forth proposals. We think that the Moroccan proposal is very serious, credible, and realistic. But in the end, we can't impose it.

Mr. WEBER. Okay, then forgive me one more question. Does the U.N. recognize Western Sahara as a what?

Mr. ROEBUCK. It is a non-self governing territory.

Mr. WEBER. A non-self governing territory.

Mr. ROEBUCK. That is the official, legal definition the U.N. uses to describe it.

Mr. WEBER. I think some might describe Congress as that. So Madame Chair, I yield back.

Ms. ROS-LEHTINEN. Thank you so much to our witnesses. Thank you to the audience, especially to our members. And with that, the subcommittee is adjourned. Thank you, ladies and gentlemen.

[Whereupon, at 4:13 p.m., the subcommittee was adjourned.]

APPENDIX

MATERIAL SUBMITTED FOR THE RECORD

SUBCOMMITTEE HEARING NOTICE
COMMITTEE ON FOREIGN AFFAIRS
U.S. HOUSE OF REPRESENTATIVES
WASHINGTON, DC 20515-6128

Subcommittee on the Middle East and North Africa
Ileana Ros-Lehtinen (R-FL), Chairman

April 2, 2014

TO: MEMBERS OF THE COMMITTEE ON FOREIGN AFFAIRS

You are respectfully requested to attend an OPEN hearing of the Committee on Foreign Affairs to be held by the Subcommittee on the Middle East and North Africa, in Room 2167 of the Rayburn House Office Building (and available live on the Committee website at www.foreignaffairs.house.gov):

DATE: Wednesday, April 9, 2014

TIME: 3:00 p.m.

SUBJECT: U.S. Policy Towards Morocco

WITNESSES: Mr. William Roebuck
                   Deputy Assistant Secretary of State for Egypt and Maghreb Affairs
                   Bureau of Near Eastern Affairs
                   U.S. Department of State

                   Ms. Alina Romanowski
                   Deputy Assistant Administrator
                   Bureau for the Middle East
                   U.S. Agency for International Development

By Direction of the Chairman

The Committee on Foreign Affairs seeks to make its facilities accessible to persons with disabilities. If you are in need of special accommodations, please call 202/225-5021 at least four business days in advance of the event, whenever practicable. Questions with regard to special accommodations in general (including availability of Committee materials in alternative formats and assistive listening devices) may be directed to the Committee.

COMMITTEE ON FOREIGN AFFAIRS

MINUTES OF SUBCOMMITTEE ON _____ *Middle East and North Africa* _____ HEARING

Day__ *Wednesday*__ Date_____ *04/09/2014*_____ Room_____ *2172*_____

Starting Time ___ *3:00 p.m.*___ Ending Time ___ *4:13 p.m.*___

Recesses ___ *0*___ (____to ____) (____to ____) (____to ____) (____to ____) (____to ____) (____to ____)

Presiding Member(s)

Chairman Ros-Lehtinen

Check all of the following that apply:

Open Session ☑
Executive (closed) Session ☐
Televised ☑

Electronically Recorded (taped) ☑
Stenographic Record ☑

TITLE OF HEARING:

U.S. Policy Toward Morocco

SUBCOMMITTEE MEMBERS PRESENT:

(See attendance sheet)

NON-SUBCOMMITTEE MEMBERS PRESENT: *(Mark with an * if they are not members of full committee.)*

* Rep. Grimm (NY)

HEARING WITNESSES: Same as meeting notice attached? Yes ☑ No ☐
(If "no", please list below and include title, agency, department, or organization.)

STATEMENTS FOR THE RECORD: *(List any statements submitted for the record.)*

None

TIME SCHEDULED TO RECONVENE _____
or
TIME ADJOURNED ___ *4:13 p.m.*___

Subcommittee Staff Director

Hearing Attendance

<u>Hearing Title</u>: U.S. Policy Toward Morocco

<u>Date</u>: 04/09/14

Noncommittee Members

Member	Present
Ros-Lehtinen, Ileana (FL)	X
Chabot, Steve (OH)	X
Wilson, Joe (SC)	
Kinzinger, Adam (IL)	X
Cotton, Tom (AR)	X
Weber, Randy (TX)	X
Desantis, Ron (FL)	
Collins, Doug (GA)	
Meadows, Mark (NC)	
Yoho, Ted (FL)	
Messer, Luke (IN)	
Grimm, Michael (NY)	

Member	Present
Deutch, Ted (FL)	X
Connolly, Gerald (VA)	X
Higgins, Brian (NY)	
Cicilline, David (RI)	
Grayson, Alan (FL)	
Vargas, Juan (CA)	
Schneider, Bradley (IL)	
Kennedy, Joseph (MA)	
Meng, Grace (NY)	
Frankel, Lois (FL)	X

www.ingramcontent.com/pod-product-compliance
Lightning Source LLC
Chambersburg PA
CBHW080635290526
45790CB00007B/3070